That [illegible]

Hazel Edwards

Illustrated by Rae Dale

The school door was open.
A bird flew in.

“Look!” said Sara.
“Where?” said the triplets.

"On the chair!" said Miss Chang.

“On my book!” said Sara. “Oh no!”
There was a white blob on Sara’s book.
The bird flew away.

Next day a bird flew in.
"Is it the same one?" asked Tom.
"Yes," said Sara.
She closed her book.

The bird flew at the window.
“It’s hurting itself,” said William.
“Can’t birds see glass?” asked Sara.

Wings flapped.
Dust floated down.

Nick opened the door.
Sara pretended to be a cat.
“Miaow,” she said.

The bird flew out, quickly!

Next day, the door was shut.
But the window was open!

That bird flew in, again.

“Use a broom,” said William.

It didn’t work.

“Use a net,” said Sara.
It almost worked.

“Let’s leave the bird alone,” said Miss Chang.
“We’ll read a bird story.”

The bird sat on top of the map.
And dropped a blob on Australia.

Next day, Miss Chang said,
"Has anyone seen that bird?"